a book about
Christopher Columbus

by RUTH BELOV GROSS

Pictures by SYD HOFF

SCHOLASTIC INC.
New York Toronto London Auckland Sydney

With appreciation to Samuel Eliot Morison

ISBN 0-590-09891-8

12 11 10 9 8 7   8 9/8 0 1 2 3/9

Printed in the U.S.A.   08

When Christopher Columbus was a little boy in Italy, he lived near the sea.

Christopher Columbus became a sailor when he was very young. He went to sea every time he had a chance.

When Columbus was about 25 years old, he went to live in a country called Portugal. He earned money in Portugal by making maps for sea captains.

The captains often talked to Columbus about the Indies. They said anyone who could sail to the Indies would get rich.

But the Indies were far away. To get there, a ship would have to sail all the way around Africa. It would be a long and dangerous voyage.

Christopher Columbus said he thought there was an easier way to get to the Indies.

Columbus told the King of Portugal about his plan. He asked the king to give him ships and men to make the voyage.

The king turned him down.

So Columbus went to ask the Queen of Spain.

When he got to Spain, he had to wait nine months just to see the queen.

Then he waited six more years for the queen to make up her mind.

First the queen said maybe.

Then the queen said no.

So Columbus decided to go to the King of France.

Then the queen changed her mind again. She sent a messenger to tell Columbus she would give him ships and men to make the voyage.

Now Columbus had to get ready.

He had to get ships.

He had to hire men and boys to sail the ships.
Some of the boys were only 12 or 13 years old.

WATER
SALT
DRIED FISH
BEANS
CHEESE
WINE
FLOUR
HONEY

He had to load the ships with enough food
for a year.

Christopher Columbus and his ships — the *Niña,* the *Pinta,* and the *Santa Maria* — left Spain on August 3, 1492. That was almost 500 years ago.

The ships stopped at some Spanish islands to fix the *Pinta* and to get more food. They stayed a month. Then they headed west to find the Indies.

On board the ships, everyone had a job to do.

The youngest boy watched the hour-glass. He was supposed to call out the time every half hour.

The sailors had one hot meal every day. The rest of the time they ate snacks — like a sardine and a cracker. Sometimes the sailors caught a fish.

The captain of each ship slept in a bunk. The
sailors slept any place they could.

No one took a bath, but sometimes the sailors
went swimming.

Every evening, they said their prayers together,
and then they all sang a hymn.

Two weeks went by. On September 25, the sailors thought they saw land — but it was only a cloud.

Another week went by. The men had never
been at sea this long before. They were sick and
tired of the whole voyage.

The men grew more and more angry. They had been sailing for a month now.

On October 10, Columbus gave them his promise. "If we do not come to the Indies in three days," he said, "we will turn back."

On October 11, the men looked up at the
sky. They looked down at the water. They saw
signs that land was near.

On the morning of October 12, 1492, the ships came to a beautiful white beach. It was an island in the Bahamas, not far from Florida.

Columbus and the officers of the three ships put on their best clothes and went ashore.

They kneeled on the ground and wept with joy.

Columbus had the feeling that there were people on the beach watching him. He was right.

He was sure he was in the Indies, so he called the people Indians.

Columbus gave the Indians some red wool caps and some glass beads and some little brass bells.

The Indians gave the sailors some parrots and some spears and some cotton thread.

They used sign language to talk to each other.

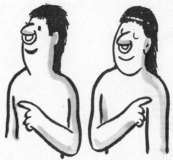

Some of the Indians had gold rings in their noses. Columbus asked the Indians where the gold came from.

And they told him.

For the next two and a half months, Columbus and his men went looking for gold.

They explored many islands and saw many
things they had never seen before —

fields of corn
sweet potatoes
big lizards
bright-colored fish
dogs that didn't bark
mockingbirds
huts with thatched roofs
hammocks
boats made out of tree trunks

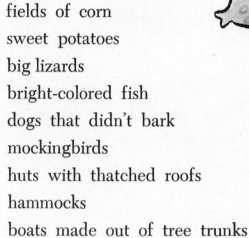

But they didn't find any gold.

Then an old man on the island of Hispaniola told Columbus where he would find gold for sure.

A few days later the ships anchored near an Indian village. More than a thousand Indians came to visit the ships.

All the Indians gave presents to the sailors. Some of the sailors got bits of gold. Columbus got the best present of all — a belt with a solid gold buckle!

It was like a party. Everybody had a good time for two days and two nights.

The party ended on December 24, 1492 — Christmas Eve. Everyone on the *Santa Maria* was very tired and went to sleep.

While they slept, the ship ran aground and was wrecked.

Christopher Columbus had only one ship now, the *Niña*. The *Pinta* had gone off to look for gold, and nobody knew where she was.

Columbus thought he'd better sail back to Spain right away. The *Niña* couldn't hold everybody, so Columbus left some of the men behind.

The men were glad. They wanted to keep looking for gold. They were hoping to find gold mines.

Columbus was sorry he had to leave before he could find pearls or spices or gold mines. But at least, he thought, he had found the Indies. To prove it, he was taking home some parrots, some plants, and a little bit of gold. Some Indians came back with him, too.

There was a terrible storm on the way back.

Columbus thought they would all be drowned.
People would never know he had found the
Indies. So he wrote a letter to the King and
Queen of Spain. He put the letter in a barrel
and threw the barrel into the sea.

Nobody ever found the barrel. But the *Niña*
reached Spain safely, and so did the *Pinta*. They
had been at sea for two months.

On March 15, 1493, Christopher Columbus was back in Spain. Now he set out for the city of Barcelona, 800 miles away, to see the king and queen.

Columbus stopped at the town where his two young sons lived. He had not seen them for eight months. He took them to Barcelona too.

The King and Queen of Spain stood up when
Christopher Columbus entered the throne room.
When he kneeled to kiss their hands, they told
him to rise and sit beside them.

They looked at all the things Columbus had brought. "You have done well," they said. "As soon as you are ready you may go back to the Indies. We will give you all the ships and men you need."

That day, Christopher Columbus was the happiest man in Spain.

What happened afterwards?

Christopher Columbus was never again as happy as on that day in Barcelona.

He went back three more times to the lands he called the Indies. He found more gold — but not a lot more. He was often short of food and supplies. Often he was ill.

He brought men from Spain to start a colony in the Indies. But he was not good at running colonies, and the men turned against him.

The King and Queen of Spain sent another man to take charge of the colony. The man arrested Columbus, and Christopher Columbus was shipped back to Spain with iron chains on his wrists and ankles.

Afterwards the king and queen were sorry. They gave Columbus permission to make his fourth voyage to the Indies. This voyage was the hardest one of all.

When Columbus came back to Spain, he was a sick man. But he wanted to go to the Indies again. He wanted to run the colony again. The king would not let him go. And the queen was dead.

Christopher Columbus became sadder and sicker and weaker. A year and a half later, at the age of 54, he died. His two sons, a few good friends, and a younger brother were at his bedside.

Christopher Columbus thought he had found the Indies. He really discovered America.

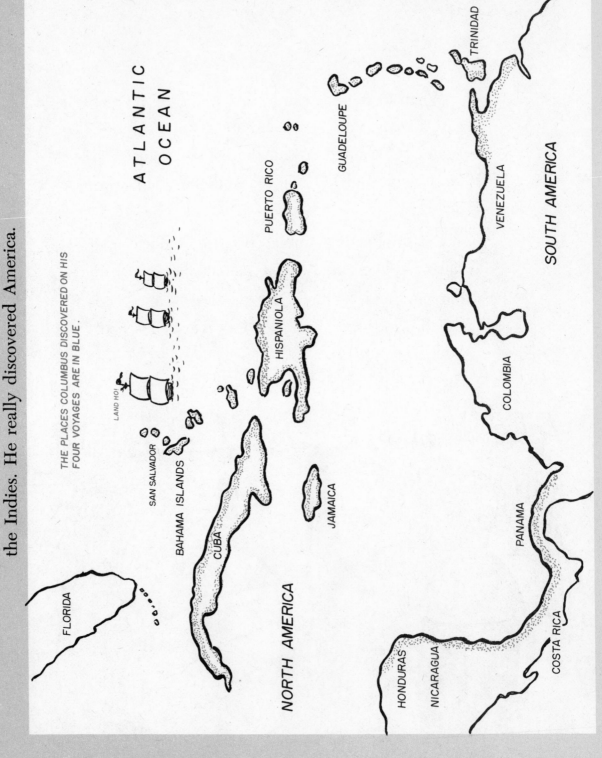

THE PLACES COLUMBUS DISCOVERED ON HIS FOUR VOYAGES ARE IN BLUE.

ATLANTIC OCEAN

FLORIDA

NORTH AMERICA

LAND HO!

SAN SALVADOR

BAHAMA ISLANDS

CUBA

JAMAICA

HISPANIOLA

PUERTO RICO

GUADELOUPE

TRINIDAD

HONDURAS

NICARAGUA

COSTA RICA

PANAMA

COLOMBIA

VENEZUELA

SOUTH AMERICA